REFLECTIVE PRAYER WITH THE PSALMS

"It is You whom I invoke, O Lord, In the morning You hear me; in the morning I offer you my prayer, watching and waiting."
(From Psalm 5)

Reflective Prayer –

Our Lord, we pray to You that our preparations be in accord with Your will. We seek Your coming in glory. We watch and wait for You to appear in radiant splendor. Come into our hearts this day.

REFLECTIVE PRAYER WITH THE PSALMS

for Advent
for Christmas

Deacon John Paul Benage

RESCRIPT

In accord with canon 826, §3, of the Code of Canon Law, I hereby grant my permission to publish *Reflective Prayer with the Psalms*, Volume 1, by Deacon John Paul Benage. This work is a collection of the author's personal reflections on the Psalms. Deacon John Paul Benage will self-publish the work.

Notice of this rescript is to be printed on the reverse side of the title page of the book.

GIVEN in San Antonio, Texas, from the Chancery Office on this the 6th day of October, 2020.

Most Reverend Gustavo García-Siller, M.Sp.S
Archbishop of San Antonio

Sister Jane Ann Slater, C.D.P.
Chancellor

SEAL

i

Psalm texts from *The Liturgy of the Hours* 1975 published by Catholic Book Publishing Corp., New York

Text of the 4 steps of *Lectio Divina* from *Workbook for Lectors, Gospel Readers and Proclaimers of the Word* 2020 published by Liturgy Training Publications, Chicago, IL

For Susan

My best friend, my love, my wife
  My partner in life

Acknowledgments

To thank everyone who contributed in some way to this book is quite possibly an impossible task. Here, I offer my sincerest gratitude to all who have supported, assisted and/or inspired this effort.

First, I thank my darling wife, Susan. Her loving support and feedback have made it possible for me to complete this task in the midst of fulfilling a myriad of other obligations and duties.

My three beautiful daughters, Yvette, Michele, and Elise provided their inputs and technical assistance with the final cover design. It is such a blessing to have young technically capable support such as these ladies.

I also offer my sincere gratitude to Bonnie Abadie at the Oblate School of Theology and my brother Deacon, Sean Dooley for their thoughtful observations, insights, and truly kind words pertaining to this effort.

And, to all who have "liked" and/or commented on these reflective prayers as they were first offered on *Facebook* over the years thank you for reading and sharing your kind words on these prayers.

Reflective Prayer with the Psalms

INTRODUCTION

Introduction

Why the Psalms?

This is no scholarly work concerning the book of Psalms. Neither is it any sort of study guide, interpretation nor discussion of these great verses. Quite simply, this is a collection of personal reflective prayers over the years.

These reflective prayers are offered here with the hope that they will stimulate further interest in these beautiful pieces. Over the years, I have seen how the Psalms have been a stumbling block for many individuals in Bible study. The most frequent complaint is, "These are too hard to understand," or simply, "I don't get this."

Reflecting on these concerns, it occurs to me that the challenge may have multiple layers. The first and most basic pertains to all scripture. Anyone who speaks more than one language knows that there are some phrases that lose much in translation. Even within a single language, there are vast differences across centuries as illustrated in the opening words of the Lord's Prayer in English today "Our Father" when compared

Reflective Prayer with the Psalms

to the Old English of the 11th century
"Faeder ure". The Psalms were written in
Ancient Hebrew probably a thousand years
before the birth of Christ on earth.

More specific to the Psalms is the style of
writing. These are written as lyrics to songs,
verse, or poetry. The lyricist or poet writes
using words as pictures. The intent is to
allow the reader to see or picture in the
mind's eye based, in part, on one's own
experiences. The words intentionally invite
new insights without detail. And, poetry,
sans the music, becomes difficult for many
to appreciate.

Thus, the Psalms are divinely inspired verse
written in an ancient language that, today,
we read in a modern language. Still, trusting
that the Church approved translations kept
intact, as much as humanly possible, the
inspired messages that invite our own new
insights into His love and call; we have a
beautiful collection of 150 Psalms to reflect
upon.

Introduction

What do you mean by *Reflective Prayer?*

For several years before I began Diaconate formation, I had a practice of reading and reflecting on scripture passages. Later, I learned of a specific prayer form, known as *Lectio Divina* (divine reading), which applied such reflection and prayer. For a great detailed description and guide to Lectio Divina you may wish to peruse the following link:

https://www.saintandrewsabbey.com/Lectio_Divina_s/267.htm

As a quick reference, the four steps of Lectio Divina are as follows:

1. *Lectio*: Read a Scripture passage aloud slowly. Notice what phrase captures your attention and be attentive to its meaning.
   After a silent pause
2. *Meditatio*: Read the passage aloud slowly again, reflecting on the passage, allowing God to speak to you through it.
   After a silent pause

3. *Oratio*: Read it aloud slowly a third time, allowing it to be your prayer or response to God's gift of insight to you.
    After a silent pause
4. *Contemplatio*: Read it aloud slowly a fourth time, now resting in God's word.

This became a form of *Reflective Prayer* for me. In formation and as a Deacon, I take up the *Liturgy of the Hours* (some of the hours) each day. Over the years, I have written down what I would take from these reflections on God's word and my response. Each is taken from a prayer hour within the *Liturgy of the Hours*, often Morning Prayer. Because all seven of the hours each day include at least two readings from the Psalms, much is available for reflection.

Few Notes on these Writings

Occasionally, there will be passages from two Psalms before the reflective prayer. In such instances, the prayer will reflect the two passages in concert with each other. Because these have been derived from multiple years, more than a single Psalm

Introduction

phrase and reflective prayer have been frequently provided for any given day.

As the Psalm phrases are taken from the *Liturgy of the Hours*, no verse references are noted therein. Noting that none of the books of the Bible had chapter and verse for several hundred years and, that the chapter numbers were added at one point while verse numbers were included some years later gave me pause as to whether or not to include verse numbers within these writings. For several reasons, I have opted to not include the verse numbers. Some of these reasons are as follows – hopefully, the interested reader will turn to the full Psalm to learn the context of the chosen verse, and perhaps the lack of verse numbers will inspire further reading of the Psalms.

In the days of the Psalm writings and for more than two millennia after there was not a system of chapter and verse of the Bible as we know it today. Ancient Israel, and most of the world's civilization well past the time of Christ were largely oral societies. Indeed, every good Jew of Jesus' day knew all 150 Psalms by heart. Each Psalm was generally known by its opening line and a message might be shared by that single line. The great example is from Jesus Himself. As He hung upon the cross, He called out, "My God, My God why have You abandoned me?" Thus, when reading Psalm 22, we see a message from our Lord for those who were present and for all humanity.

Overall, the hope here is that this will, in some small way, both aid those who find it difficult to study the Psalms while encouraging all readers to reflect more deeply on these verses that are called the prayer of the Church.

Reflective Prayer with the Psalms

ADVENT

For Advent

First Sunday of Advent ~

Psalm 2 concludes: "Blessed are they who put their trust in God."

Reflective Prayer –

O Lord, our God, on this first Sunday of Advent, we prepare for His coming. When your son comes in glory, may we have prepared according to your will.

Our trust is in you, O Lord our God, who made heaven and earth. May our trust in you be our guide in preparing for His coming to be our judge.

"For your love is better than life, my lips will speak your praise." (From Psalm 63)

Reflective Prayer –

Your love, O Lord our God, is shown most clearly on the cross. This passion you have shown to us and for us is the sign of your love. Lord help us to focus on the cross as your love for us, that it may become our love for you in others we serve.

O wonderous and infinite God, we have no means to know your complete love for us! All that you do and all that you are is far beyond our understanding. Trusting always in your love, we ask you to wrap us in your guiding hands all of our days. May our lives reflect only love for you and all that you have created.

For Advent

Monday of the First Week ~

"It is you whom I invoke, O Lord. In the morning you hear me; in the morning I offer you my prayer, watching and waiting." (From Psalm 5)

Reflective Prayer –

Our Lord, we pray to you that our preparations be in accord with your will. We seek your coming in glory. We watch and wait for you to appear in radiant splendor. Come into our hearts this day.

———

"I bow down before your holy temple, filled with awe." (From Psalm 5)

Reflective Prayer –

Your power and might, we cannot perceive, O Lord. You are the Creator of all, and everything continues to be at your desire alone. Made in your image and likeness, we are called to love as you love. Give us, then, pure hearts for such love that we may do your will alone.

Reflective Prayer with the Psalms

Tuesday of the First Week ~

Psalm 24 begins, "The Lord's is the earth and its fullness, the world and all its peoples."

Reflective Prayer—

We are yours, O Lord, in all things and at all times. We place our lives in your hands, trusting you in all things. Your unconditional love sustains us always. May our lives reflect your love in your law.

———

"O gates, lift high your heads; grow higher ancient doors. Let Him enter, the King of glory." (From Psalm 24)

Reflective Prayer –

Lord God, heavenly King, guide our hearts and minds to know and do your will. Grant us the grace that we may lift up our heads and open the doors of our hearts.

With minds and hearts opened to your will; with loving hands doing your work; with faithful voices proclaiming your word; and, with feet set firmly on your way may we prepare all we must for your coming in glory.

———

For Advent

Psalm 33 concludes, "May your love be upon us, O Lord, as we place all our hope in you."

Reflective Prayer –

Watching and waiting for your coming in glory, O Lord; we hope in you alone. Guide our hearts and minds to your peace as we share the good news in service to others.

Reflective Prayer with the Psalms

Wednesday of the First Week ~

"It is He who set it on the seas; on the waters He made it firm." (From Psalm 24)

Reflective Prayer –

You have given us the land for our use and livelihood, O God. Yet, we abuse it and scar it for worthless pleasures. Forgive our abuses, Lord. We pray that we may always turn to you and live only in your love. Guide our hearts and minds to share our gifts and talents with those in need of these.

––––––––

"Sin speaks to the sinner in the depths of his heart. There is no fear of God before his eyes…All wisdom is gone.

O Lord, how precious is your love…Keep on loving those who know you, doing justice for upright hearts." (From Psalm 36)

Reflective Prayer –

We know you, O Lord, in our hearts and in the depths of our souls. We know you are love. Bind us in your light and love that we may lead others to you.

For Advent

Thursday of the First Week ~

"Who shall climb the mountain of the Lord?" (From Psalm 24)

Reflective Prayer –

To see you, Lord, with the eyes of our hearts; to hear your word with the ears of our soul; to pray with all of our being is to know you here on earth, O Lord our God. Knowing you and loving you in your commandments; and loving all others as ourselves, this is to climb your mountain to walk in your path, O Lord. Guide our steps this day.

———

"O God, we ponder your love within your temple. Your praise, O God, like your name reaches the ends of the earth." (From Psalm 48)

Reflective Prayer –

Your love for us, O God, is unfathomable. It is beyond all understanding. You, who are without limits, came to your creation that had turned its back on you. You humbled yourself to become one of us that you might reconcile us to yourself. Help us to see your great love in our hearts and welcome your rebirth there. Guide us to be ready when you come again in glory.

Reflective Prayer with the Psalms

Friday of the First Week ~

"Who shall stand in His holy place?" (From Psalm 24)

Reflective Prayer –

We long to see your face, O God! To praise you all of our days! Yet, no one of this world can look upon your glory and live. Take from us then, O God, our stony hearts filled with earthly desires. Grant us hearts for you alone that we might be pure of heart, mind, and soul – pleasing to you. And, by your grace alone, may we stand in your holy place for ever.

———

"A pure heart create in me, O God, put a steadfast spirit within me." (From Psalm 51)

Reflective Prayer –

We pray to you, O Lord, that we might prepare ourselves to welcome you at your re-birth in our hearts; that your re-birth as our savior might make our hearts pure; that we might look for your coming in glory with great joy.

For Advent

Saturday of the First Week ~

"Consider the Lord and His strength; constantly seek His face." (From Psalm 105)

Reflective Prayer –

Lord, our God, your strength gives us life. Without you we are not. We praise you and thank you for your glory, for all that you have done for humanity. Grant us the grace to always know and do your will.

———

"I rise before dawn and cry for help, I hope in your word. My eyes watch through the night to ponder your promise" (From Psalm 119)

Reflective Prayer –

Lord God, we watch and wait for your coming. Come and rescue us from our afflictions and addictions to sin. Open our hearts that we may welcome your redemptive grace as renewed birth in us. Guide us to lead lives that produce good fruit for eternity as we await your coming in glory.

———

"The man with clean hands and pure heart, who desires not worthless things, who has not sworn so as to deceive his neighbor." (From Psalm 24)

Reflective Prayer with the Psalms

"In your love hear my voice, O Lord; give me life by your decrees." (From Psalm 119)

Reflective Prayer –

Place a clean heart in each of us, O Lord, that we may desire as you would have us. Make our lives a walk in your light to see you in every soul we meet. May our hearts and our tongue offer only your truth.

For Advent

Second Sunday of Advent ~

*H*e shall receive blessings from the Lord and reward from the God who saves him. (From Psalm 24)

"O Lord grant us salvation; O Lord, grant success." (From Psalm 118)

Reflective Prayer –

May all our being bless, praise and please you, O Lord, that in your mercy, you might grant us salvation.

Reflective Prayer with the Psalms

Monday of the Second Week ~

"Why are you cast down, my soul, why groan within me? Hope in God: I will praise Him still, my savior and my God." (From Psalm 42)

Reflective Prayer –

All our hope is in you O Lord, our God. You have the way to everlasting life. You are our comfort and joy.

Let us turn our hearts and minds to you alone that we may never be cast down. Trusting in you, may we always know light and life.

———

"Such are the men who seek Him, seek the face of the God of Jacob." (From Psalm 24)

"For your love is better than life, my lips will speak your praise." (From Psalm 63)

Reflective Prayer –

Look upon us with your mercy, O God. We seek your face as the only worthwhile goal. Still, in our flesh we are weak and fail to love you always. But your love is complete and unconditional. Guide our hearts to love as you love.

———

For Advent

"For the Lord takes delight in His people. He crowns the poor with salvation." (From Psalm 149)

Reflective Prayer –

Grant that we may always be your delight, O Lord, in all our thoughts, words and actions. May we always show each other mercy and thus, receive your mercy.

Reflective Prayer with the Psalms

Tuesday of the Second Week ~

"O send forth your light and your truth; let these be my guide. Let them bring me to your holy mountain, to the place where you dwell." (From Psalm 43)

Reflective Prayer –

Holy Spirit, source of light, shine forth upon us today. Enlighten our hearts with your seven holy gifts. Open our hearts to your truth.

In pure truth that is you, O God, may we come to the abode of your dwelling. There may we know eternal joy with you.

———

"O gates, lift high your heads; grow higher, ancient doors. Let Him enter, the King of glory!" (From Psalm 24)

"Blessed is he whom you choose and call to dwell in your courts." (From Psalm 65)

Reflective Prayer –

You call each of us, Lord. But we must receive your call and welcome you into our hearts. Our joy is complete when we abide in your eternal love.

For Advent

Wednesday of the Second Week ~

"Who is the King of glory? The Lord, the mighty, the valiant, the Lord, the valiant in war." (From Psalm 24)

Psalm 97 begins: "The Lord is king, let the earth rejoice, let all the coastlands be glad."

Reflective Prayer –

You, O Lord, are our protector and shield in the spiritual war waging across our land. The forces of darkness and evil have invaded the very fabric of our nation, calling evil good and good evil. Yet, your faithful know your grace and trust in your love.

We know you will triumph over all evil and save the souls who hold out to the end. Come to our aid and let our hearts not be troubled but, look to your coming in glory.

———

Psalm 113 begins, "Praise, O servants of the Lord, praise the name of the Lord! May the name of the Lord be blessed both now and for evermore!"

Reflective Prayer –

What a generous gift you have given us, O Lord our God! That we might praise your name.

Reflective Prayer with the Psalms

To know you is to love you, and in that love is our gift – the chance to praise you for your glory. And you receive our praise O Lord our God!

For Advent

Thursday of the Second Week ~

(For the Solemnity of the Immaculate Conception)

The antiphon within Psalm 46 reads, "The Lord of hosts is with us: the God of Jacob is our stronghold."

Reflective Prayer –

As we contemplate your coming O Lord, we pray, "O come, O come Emanuel (God with us)". How beautiful is our prayer this day as we commemorate the Immaculate Conception of your holy mother the woman that would be the vessel of your birth to us.

Your holy mother, that you gave to us, brought forth Emanuel. We celebrate her Immaculate Conception in preparation of your being with us!

———

"A voice I did not know said to me; 'I freed your shoulder from the burden; your hands were freed from the load. You called in distress and I saved you.'" (From Psalm 81)

Reflective Prayer –

Lord, you save us from our own wickedness, from our sinful ways and, our evil desires when we call to you and name our wrongful ways. Jesus, we trust in you, aid our unbelief.

Reflective Prayer with the Psalms

(For the Feast of Our Lady of Guadalupe)

O gates, lift high your heads; grow higher, ancient doors. (From Psalm 24)

Psalm 81 begins, "Ring out you joy to God our strength shout in triumph to the God of Jacob."

Reflective Prayer –

Our joy is beyond our means of expression, O God! We open the gates of our hearts to you that you might enter and fill us with your peace. No evil can move us from our joy in you. In your grace, we know our eternal home awaits.

For Advent

Friday of the Second Week ~

"Let Him enter, the King of glory." (From Psalm 24)

"Make me hear rejoicing and gladness, that the bones you have crushed may revive." (From Psalm 51)

Reflective Prayer –

Come to us, O Lord, in your glory! Our King and our God enter into the hearts of our souls that we may live in your love and mercy. Cleanse us from our inequities that we may welcome you as you come in glory.

———

Psalm 38 concludes, "O Lord, do not forsake me! My God, do not stay afar off! Make haste and come to help, O Lord, my God, my Savior!

Reflective Prayer –

Our pleadings for your help, O Lord, are unceasing. Day and night, we call to you. Guard us from the temptations that beseech us and from a world that seeks our ruin. Our trust is in you alone, O Lord, our God.

———

Reflective Prayer with the Psalms

"My help shall come from the Lord who made heaven and earth." (From Psalm 121)

Reflective Prayer –

You are indeed our help and salvation O Lord our God. You strengthen us in our hour of need and comfort us in sorrow. It is you and you alone, O God, who is our love, our life, and our salvation. Grant us your grace as we prepare for your coming.

For Advent

Saturday of the Second Week ~

"When I see the heavens, the work of your hands, the moon and the stars which you arranged, what is man that you should keep him in mind, mortal man that you care for him?" (From Psalm 8)

Reflective Prayer –

We praise you, O Lord our God, for you have great love and care for us! Though we are lowly feeble, stubborn, and often unwilling to listen to and follow your Word, you love each of us and call us to return to you.

There is no greater love than you. Guide us with your grace to always follow your law.

———

"…what is man that you should keep him in mind…Yet you have made him little less than a god; with glory and honor you crowned him, gave him power over the works of your hand, put all things under his feet." (From Psalm 8)

Reflective Prayer –

All this you have given us, O Lord! And yet, we abuse your gifts. We are unworthy stewards of your gifts, debasing them for our own satisfaction and gain. Forgive our abuses Lord, guide us to your will in all things that we may know your joy always.

———

"Who is the King of glory?" (From Psalm 24)

"He crowns the poor with salvation." (From Psalm 149)

Reflective Prayer –

Humbly we come before you, O God. We acknowledge our weakness of spirit and poverty of knowledge with respect to the things of heaven. And you seek out the poor of our world – those who suffer out of love of you. May your grace move us to embrace these, your children and, thus, learn of your eternal joy through humble hearts.

For Advent

Third Sunday of Advent ~

*G*reater than the roar of mighty waters, more glorious than the surging of the sea, the Lord is glorious on high. (From Psalm 93)

Reflective Prayer –

Your glory abounds O Lord! We praise you now and forever. May we be ever in your presence, knowing your peace and joy!

———

Psalm 148 begins, "Praise the Lord from the heavens, praise Him in the heights."

Reflective Prayer –

With all the hosts of heaven, we praise you, O Lord our God! You came into the world out of pure love to redeem your creation. Come now, long expected Jesus come in your glory.

———

Psalm 148 concludes, "He exalts the strength of His people. He is the praise of all His saints, of the sons of Israel, of the people to whom He comes close."

Reflective Prayer –

Reflective Prayer with the Psalms

Lord guide us in our journey on this earth. Show us the way to you. Help us to see you in every soul on the earth.

Seeing you in every soul and greeting, helping, strengthening each soul here, may we be amongst those to whom you come. In your grace and peace, may we know your strength in us and rejoice in our love of you.

For Advent

Monday of the Third Week ~

Psalm 24 concludes, "He, the Lord of armies, He is the King of glory."

"One day in your courts is better than a thousand elsewhere." (From Psalm 84)

Reflective Prayer –

You are the King of our hearts, O Lord! Lead us in this spiritual battle that wages against your law. Come, O Lord our God, bring us to your courts, our eternal home.

Reflective Prayer with the Psalms

Tuesday of the Third Week –

Psalm 11 concludes, "The Lord is just and loves justice: the upright shall see His face."

Reflective Prayer –

Lord God look upon your broken people and have mercy on us. Open the eyes of our hearts to the justice that is you. May the ears of our hearts hear only your commands.

Grant us gentle hearts, O God, that know your mercy and love; then, may we act with your justice toward all. There we will see your face.

———

Psalm 67 begins, "O God, be gracious and bless us and let your face shed its light upon us."

Psalm 95 begins, "Come, let us sing to the Lord and shout with joy to the Rock who saves us."

Reflective Prayer –

Your ways, O Lord, are truth and light. Grant us the grace to share your ways with a world draped in darkness and death; that, joy may spring upon a troubled people.

Your blessings upon us abound, O Lord our God! For these, we give you thanks and praise all our days. The light of your face guides us along our journey home to you. Your grace abounds upon us. You are our Rock who saves us.

————

"Truly I have set my soul in silence and peace. As a child has rest in its mother's arms, even so is my soul." (From Psalm 131)

Reflective Prayer –

We rest in you, O Lord our God, for you are our strength, our salvation and life. We turn to you and you heal all our sinfulness in your loving arms. Now, we praise you as we prepare to welcome Jesus come to earth as King.

Reflective Prayer with the Psalms

Wednesday of the Third Week ~

"O Lord, arise in your strength; we shall sing and praise your power." (From Psalm 21)

Reflective Prayer –

You give your strength to all who praise your name and believe in you, O Lord! Let us reign in each other's hearts as your servants. Caring for every soul in this way, we sing your praises as we witness the real power of your love.

————

"So will your face be known upon earth and all nations learn your saving help." (From Psalm 67)

"The Lord has made known His salvation; has shown His justice to the nations." (From Psalm 98)

Reflective Prayer –

All nations will know you, O Lord, know your saving help, your justice and mercy. For your unconditional love knows all things and searches the hearts of every soul. In your great mercy, Lord, forgive our transgressions and bring each soul to a just state before you. In this state, may we come to our home with you.

For Advent

Thursday of the Third Week ~

"Let the peoples praise you, O God; let all the peoples praise you." (From Psalm 67)

"It is He, the Most High, who gives each his place." (From Psalm 87)

Reflective Prayer –

O gracious and all-knowing God, you are our source of all being. Knowing that you have made each soul conceived on the earth with a place and purpose in your divine design, we ask you to guide us through the struggles of our lives that we might fulfill your will for each of us. Doing your will is the highest praise we can offer you.

———

Psalm 99 concludes, "Exalt the Lord our God; bow down before His holy mountain for the Lord our God is holy."

Reflective Prayer –

You are holy indeed O Lord our God! Our lives are blessed and made holy only when we receive you. Apart from you, there is nothing. In you we know joy in our suffering and peace in a troubled land. Help us to joyfully receive you daily.

Reflective Prayer with the Psalms

Friday of the Third Week ~

"He shall receive blessings from the Lord and reward from the God who saves him. Such are the men who seek Him, seek the face of the God of Jacob." (From Psalm 24)

Reflective Prayer –

Guide us to seek your face in all we think; in all we say, and, in all we do O Lord our God. Your blessings upon us will bring everlasting joy.

———

"My offenses truly I know them; my sin is always before me. Against you, you alone, have I sinned; what is evil in your sight I have done…

Indeed you love truth in the heart; then in the secret of my heart teach me wisdom. O purify me, then I shall be clean, O wash me, I shall be whiter than snow…

O rescue me, God, my helper, and my tongue shall ring out your goodness." (From Psalm 51)

Reflective Prayer –

Preparing our hearts for your coming in glory, Lord, forgive our sins as we confess them with contrite hearts. Then we shall truly know your peace.

For Advent

"Let the nations be glad and exult for you rule the world with justice." (From Psalm 67)

"O Lord, open my lips and my mouth shall declare your praise" (From Psalm 51)

We praise you, O Lord, for your justice and mercy. We exult in your loving grace! May your way become our way all of our days. For it is your love that has brought us our redemption, Jesus the Christ.

Reflective Prayer with the Psalms

Saturday of the Third Week ~

"With fairness you rule the peoples, you guide the nations on earth." (From Psalm 67)

Psalm 117 begins, "O praise the Lord all you nations, acclaim Him all you peoples."

Reflective Prayer –

You guide the nations O God. Yet, in our wayward will we lose our path. Shine your light on us who have strayed from the road to you. In Him, who is the Way, the Truth, and the Light, may all peoples of all nations journey together to our home in you.

———

"My heart and my flesh cry out for the living God." (From Psalm 84)

Reflective Prayer –

To be with you, O God, is the great desire of every heart. Among us are many who do not know this; many who do not know you; and some who deny you. Yet all of us live at your will and are lacking in joy apart from you.

We watch and wait for you to come and reside with us always. Come, O Lord, and do not delay.

For Advent

Fourth Sunday of Advent ~

*L*et the peoples praise you, O God; let all the
peoples praise you. *(From Psalm 67)*

Psalm 118 begins, "Give thanks to the Lord
for He is good, for His love endures forever."

Reflective Prayer –

Praise and thanksgiving to you, O Lord our God!
You have given us life – life in your image and
likeness. You have redeemed us from our own
transgressions and granted us grace ant the promise
of eternal life with you! Our joy is complete, living
in your peace and love of each soul you set upon the
earth.

———

"This day was made by the Lord; we rejoice and are
glad." (From Psalm 118)

Reflective Prayer –

Lord our God, you are all in all. As this day and
every day, you are in everything and everything is
of you.

We praise you for your glory and give you thanks
for this day,

for our joy in suffering out of love of you, for our life in service of you in all those we meet, and for your great love of all humanity. May we each bring another heart to you on this beautiful day.

For Advent

Monday of the Fourth Week ~

"The earth has yielded its fruit for God, our God, has blessed us." (From Psalm 67)

"Make us know the shortness of our life that we may gain wisdom of heart." (From Psalm 90)

Reflective Prayer –

Your gifts of grace and blessing are always upon us, Lord. Yet we must accept these to receive them. Open in us those places we have kept closed to your grace that we may live only for you in each soul we meet.

———

"I was stupid and did not understand, no better than a beast in your sight. Yet I was always in your presence; you were holding me by my right hand. You will guide me by your counsel and so lead me to glory." (From Psalm 73)

Reflective Prayer –

How can we believe that we know what is best? Why do we try to do it our own way? Riches and pleasures of the world pass and give no joy.

In your law, in you alone is our joy. Lead us each day of our lives, O Lord, that we may walk eternally in your light and your everlasting joy!

Reflective Prayer with the Psalms

Tuesday of the Fourth Week ~

(For Christmas Eve)

Psalm 67 concludes, "May God still give us His blessing till the ends of the earth revere Him."

"I will walk in the way of perfection. O when, Lord will you come?" (From Psalm 101)

Reflective Prayer –

Striving always to do your will, O Lord, we seek your continued blessing. Come then Lord Jesus and, in our souls this day, melt our hearts into thine.

———

Psalm 101 begins, "My song is of mercy and justice; I sing to you, O Lord. I will walk in the way of perfection. O when, Lord, will you come?"

Reflective Prayer --

Help us to show mercy to one another Lord, that we may know your mercy – for in your mercy is true justice known. Come, O Lord, bring us your mercy and love.

———

"Reach down from heaven and save me; draw me out from the might waters, from the hands of alien

For Advent

foes where mouths are filled with lies, whose hands are raised in perjury." (From Psalm 144)

Reflective Prayer --

Our foes surround us on every side, O Lord. They come from near and far, even from within. Some we know but others we do not even see. Guide and protect us on our journey to you that we may not stray from your course and law, not succumb to seductions and false teachings but live only in your love.

Reflective Prayer with the Psalms

Wednesday of the Fourth Week ~

Psalm 139 begins, "O Lord, you search me and you know me. You know my resting and my rising, you decern my purpose from afar. You mark when I walk or lie down, all my ways lie open to you."

Reflective Prayer –

You know each of us better than we know ourselves, O Lord, our God. Before we form a tiny thought, you know it.

You abhor lies because these oppose truth, and you are truth itself. We are unable to hide anything from you. This is a great truth in which we should rejoice. For knowing that you know us better than we know ourselves brings solace, as your forgiveness is unfathomable in our hearts.

For Advent

Thursday of the Fourth Week ~

"Teach me to do your will for you, O Lord, are my God." (From Psalm 143)

Reflective Prayer –

As we come close to completing our time of preparation, Lord we turn to you for clear direction. Shine your light of truth upon us. In your wisdom, direct our lives.

God of mercy, truth, and justice teach us to prepare always for our coming before you. May our days and nights all be lived in your will.

Reflective Prayer with the Psalms

Friday of the Fourth Week ~

(For Christmas Eve) "

Teach me to do your will for you, O Lord, are my God…For your name's sake, Lord, save my soul from distress." (From Psalm 143)

Reflective Prayer –

Help us, O God, to form our hearts and minds to yours. May we know your heart as our heart and your desire as our desire. Save us from the false pleasures of this world.

———

"He has strengthened the bars of your gates, He has blessed the children within you. He established peace on your borders, He feeds you with finest wheat." (From Psalm 147)

Reflective Prayer –

Our world struggles to find peace, O Lord. Our youth are indeed blessed, but often confused. Peace on our borders is tenuous and disrupted by violence. And we often fail to feed our hungry among us. Grant your faithful the peace this world cannot give. Guide our youth to find the truth that is you. Teach us to show love for all humanity in the breaking and sharing of bread. And, through your son, bring peace to all the earth.

For Advent

Saturday of the Fourth Week ~

(For Christmas Eve)

P salm 8 begins, "How great is your name, O Lord our God, through all the earth!"

Reflective Prayer –

Your name, O God, is beyond our understanding. You are all in all. Apart from you, there is nothing. And yet, you come to save us mortal beings from our own wicked ways. Praise be your name forever.

CHRISTMAS

For Christmas

The First Day ~ December 25th

P salm 100 begins, "Cry out with joy to the Lord, all the earth."

"My soul shall be filled as with a banquet, my mouth shall praise you with joy." (From Psalm 63)

Reflective Prayer –

Filled with the joy of knowing you became man for our salvation, we are overcome with joy this day O Lord our God! The joy we know this happy morning fills the hearts of our souls. May we share our joy with all humanity.

———

"I will announce the decree of the Lord: The Lord said to me! You are my son. It is I who have begotten you this day. Ask and I shall bequeath you the nations, put the ends of the earth in your possession." (From Psalm 2)

Reflective Prayer –

What greater gift can our Creator give than eternal life? This day, we thank you, O Lord, our God for the gift of your Son, our salvation.

———

Reflective Prayer with the Psalms

"You are the fairest of the children of men and graciousness is poured upon your lips: because God has blessed you for evermore." (From Psalm 45)

Reflective Prayer –

The Psalmist praises a king. But you, O Lord, our God, have made each of us who receive you in baptism, sharers of your kingship. You have come amongst us today to redeem our fallen nature. Grant us grace to follow you in your love for all and in your law.

For Christmas

The Second Day ~ December 26th

"Come before Him, singing for joy." (From Psalm 100)

Psalm 149 begins, "Sing a new song to the Lord, His praise in the assembly of the faithful."

Reflective Prayer –

Praising you, O Lord, our God, is a joy that swells up from the depths of our soul. As the Holy Spirit prays for us with sighs too deep for words, such is our joy in praising you for your coming to earth as our Redeemer.

––––––

"O God, you are my God, for you I long; for you my soul is thirsting…For your love is better than life, my lips will speak your praise." (From Psalm 63)

Reflective Prayer –

Lord teach us love; the love that is you, O my God. We know not love if we do not know you. Send us *Wisdom* that she might teach us how to choose love of you in each other every day.

––––––

Psalm 95 begins, "Come, let us sing to the Lord and shout with joy to the Rock who saves us."

Reflective Prayer with the Psalms

Reflective Prayer –

You, who have created us, have come down as a child among us. O Lord, you have humbled yourself to redeem an unfaithful people. Creator of all that exists, power of the universe, and glorified by all the citizens of heaven, you became one of us to redeem us from our sins.

No song, no praise, no acclaim that we can give to you would ever be enough. Let us offer these at every moment of every day in all that we think, do, and say.

———

Psalm 100 concludes, "Indeed, how good is the Lord, eternal His merciful love. He is faithful from age to age."

Reflective Prayer –

Would that we were always faithful to you, O Lord, our God. Your unconditional love grants us a boundless mercy when we turn to you with contrite hearts. Praise to you, O Lord Jesus Christ now and forever!

For Christmas

The Third Day ~ December 27th

"Know that He, the Lord, is God." (From Psalm 100)

"O God, you are my God, for you I long; for you my soul is thirsting." (From Psalm 63)

Reflective Prayer –

O Lord, our Creator, our Redeemer, our home, grant us the grace of salvation. You are God alone. We seek always to be with you. But, to do so, we must do your will here on the earth. Doing your will is loving you; and only such pure love will bring us home to you. Grant us guidance and grace on our journey.

———

Psalm 95 begins: "Come, let us sing to the Lord and shout with joy to the Rock who saves us."

Reflective Prayer –

Lord, you are our Rock. You alone can save us from our evil inclinations. Your grace is enough. Help us to willingly accept your gift of grace and cooperate with it through works of mercy.

———

"For the Lord takes delight in His people. He crowns the poor with salvation." (From Psalm 149)

Reflective Prayer with the Psalms

Reflective Prayer –

Lord, you love the poor. Show us, who are poor in spirit, humbled before you; we seek your mercy and love. Grant that we may always be your people in all we think, in our every act, and in each word that we speak.

For Christmas

The Fourth Day ~ December 28th

"He made us, we belong to Him, we are His people, the sheep of His flock." (From Psalm 100)

"For the Lord takes delight in His peoples." (From Psalm 149)

Reflective Prayer –

Our joy is in living as you created us. Your love for us, beyond all our understanding or imagining, calls us to live in your law and love. It is your law that is there for our joy.

Seeking our own desires and pleasures without regard for your other children darkens the hearts of our souls and brings us confusion and loss. Fill us with your grace and blessings, O Lord, that we may never stray from your way for us.

———

"Our soul is waiting for the Lord. The Lord is our help and our shield." (From Psalm 33)

Reflective Prayer –

Protect us, O Lord, from the lures and allurements of this world. Guide us and inform our hearts so that we know what is pure, what is just and what is true according to your Word, O God.

———

Reflective Prayer with the Psalms

"O God, you are my God, for you I long; for you my soul is thirsting." (From Psalm 63)

Reflective Prayer –

We seek you in our journey home, O Lord. Keep us in your way, on your path; that our longing be not in vain.

As the holy innocents were sacrificed out of worldly power, may our sacrifices in support of the unborn be pleasing to you and bring us closer to our eternal home with you.

———

"For your love is better than life, my lips will speak your praise. So I will bless you all my life in your name I will lift up my hands." (From Psalm 63)

Reflective Prayer –

Nothing is greater than praising you, O Lord, our God. For you have made us from nothing out of Your great love. May we always praise you in all we think, say, and do.

For Christmas

The Fifth Day ~ December 29th

"Go within His gates, giving thanks." (From Psalm 100)

"For your love is better than life, my lips will speak your praise." (From Psalm 63)

Reflective Prayer –

We give you thanks and praise always, O Lord, our God. For you have sent us a Redeemer, your Son, Jesus the Christ. With Mary and Joseph to help form Him in humanity, He is fully God and fully man forever. What greater love could our Creator show His creation, God with us!

————

"God is for us a refuge and strength, a helper close at hand in time of distress...'Be still and know that I am God, supreme among the nations, supreme on the earth!'" (From Psalm 46)

Reflective Prayer –

Father, we know there is no crown of glory without our effort and trial. In our struggles, we turn to you – our refuge and strength. Help us to quiet our minds and hearts so as to be attuned to the softness of your voice that comforts and assures.

————

Reflective Prayer with the Psalms

"From oppression He will rescue their lives, to Him their blood is dear." (From Psalm 72)

Reflective Prayer –

Today, we know oppression upon many of your creation, O Lord. Many are oppressed by acts of war and violence, many by physical and mental abuse, and others by government and social oppression for what they believe.

We ask your grace for each of these who are oppressed. May your grace strengthen and enliven us. May we embrace our afflictions through your grace to win the crown of glory that you hold out for each of us.

For Christmas

The Sixth Day ~ December 30th

"Enter His courts with songs of praise." (From Psalm 100)

"Let the faithful rejoice in their glory." (From Psalm 149)

Reflective Prayer –

You, O Lord, are our glory! Knowing you in your love for us, we receive your blessing and grace. Living in your joy amid suffering and sacrifice, we look forward to entering your gates in eternal joy and glory.

———

"I will hear what the Lord God has to say, a voice that speaks of peace, peace for His people and His friends and those who turn to Him in their hearts." (From Psalm 85)

Reflective Prayer –

Guide us to the stillness of mind and heart O Lord, that we might hear your voice. Listening with our hearts, may we drive out all our selfish desires and seek your peace within.

———

"I will sing for ever of your love, O Lord; through all ages my mouth will proclaim your truth. Of this

Reflective Prayer with the Psalms

I am sure, that your love lasts for ever, that your truth is firmly established as the heavens." (From Psalm 89)

Reflective Prayer –

O Lord, our God, your love is truth and beyond your truth there is none. Guide us always in your truth, that we may love all humanity as your children.

For Christmas

The Seventh Day ~ December 31st

"Give thanks to Him and bless His name." (From Psalm 100)

"My soul clings to you; your right hand holds me fast." (From Psalm 63)

Reflective Prayer –

Your name, O Lord, is forever glorious, for you are our hope and salvation! All things are possible with you and in you. Apart from you we can do nothing.

In our eternal thanks to you, we seek your face. May we each be found worthy of eternal life with you.

———

Psalm 87 begins, "On the holy mountain is His city cherished by the Lord. The Lord prefers the gates of Zion to all Jacob's dwellings. Of you are told glorious things, O city of God!"

Reflective Prayer –

Lord and Savior, coming to earth, you formed a Holy Family with Mary and Joseph. What city could be more holy than that wherein you dwell, where Mary and Joseph reside with you forever? Guide us to your holy dwelling, we pray.

Reflective Prayer with the Psalms

Psalm 113 begins, "Praise, O servants of the Lord, praise the name of the Lord! May the name of the Lord be blessed both now and forever more!"

Reflective Prayer –

We praise you, O God, and know that we will know the joy of your word and be on guard against evil by truly praising you. In this, we are blessed, not knowing whence you come – neither the day nor the hour.

"From the rising of the sun to its setting praised be the name of the Lord!" (From Psalm 113)

Reflective Prayer –

Our praise is due you, O Lord our God, always and in everything. As the year draws to a close, we thank you for every blessing, for every trial that brings us grace to see it through, for every challenge that strengthened our faith in you, for those times we suffered in your name to receive grace upon grace, and for all the joy you have bestowed on us through those whom we have loved.

Praise to You Lord Jesus Christ now and forever!

For Christmas

The Eighth Day ~ *Solemnity of Mary Mother of God* ~ January 1st

*I*ndeed, how good is the Lord, eternal His merciful love. (From Psalm 100)

"He crowns the poor with salvation." (From Psalm 149)

Reflective Prayer –

Jesus, our King, born of the Virgin Mary, gave her to us as our mother on the cross as you died for our sins. In your eternal mercy, grant each of us poor sinners eternal life with you. Mary, Virgin Mother, pray for each of us and our salvation.

———

"Who shall climb the mountain of the Lord? Who shall stand in His holy place?

The man with clean hands and a pure heart, who desires not worthless things, who has not sworn so as to deceive his neighbor." (From Psalm 24)

Reflective Prayer –

A pure heart create in us O God, that we might know and do your will with hands cleansed in your love.

Reflective Prayer with the Psalms

Mary, mother of God, pure and humble of heart O pray for us.

———

Psalm 99 concludes, "Exalt the Lord our God; bow down before His holy mountain for the Lord our God is holy."

Reflective Prayer –

"And Mary said: 'My soul proclaims the greatness of the Lord, my spirit rejoices in God my Savior for He has looked with favor on His lowly Servant.

From this day all generations will call me blessed: the Almighty has done great things for me, and holy is His Name.'" Luke 1:46-49

And we say: "Holy Mary, Mother of God, pray for us sinners now and at the hour of our death."

———

Psalm 127 begins, "If the Lord does not build the house in vain do its builders labor."

Reflective Prayer –

What a house you have built for us on earth, O Lord our God! Your Church not made of stones but souls – millions of souls! She is our guide on this pilgrim journey to our eternal home with you.

For Christmas

May we always remain true to Her teaching which comes from your Holy Spirit.

On this Solemnity of your holy mother, let us honor her as our mother and model for your Church.

Reflective Prayer with the Psalms

The Ninth Day ~ January 2nd

Psalm 100 concludes, "He is faithful from age to age."

"So I will bless you all my life, in your name I will lift up my hands." (From Psalm 63)

Reflective Prayer –

In our youth, we praise you, O Lord. As we grow in our faith and love for you, we praise you. At the extended years of our days on earth, we praise you. For you are faithful to each soul created in your image and likeness all of our days.

———

Psalm 6 concludes, "Leave me, all you who do evil; for the Lord has heard my weeping. The Lord has heard my plea; the Lord will accept my prayer. All my foes will retire in confusion, foiled and suddenly confounded."

Psalm 67 begins, "O God be gracious and bless us."

Reflective Prayer –

Lord, your broken people seek your face. Opening our broken bodies, our dejected minds, our downtrodden spirits and hate-filled hearts to your loving kindness and mercy; we beg you to heal and defend us from the eternal enemy. Trusting in your love and mercy, we find true joy and peace.

————

Psalm 54 begins, "O God, save me by your name; by your power uphold my cause."

Reflective Prayer –

We are surrounded by unbelief; taunted by evil doers; and, challenged by those who call good evil and evil good. Our strength is in you alone, O Lord our God. Send forth your Spirit to guide and aide us in your grace.

————

Psalm 92 begins: "It is good to give thanks to the Lord to make music to your name, O most High…"

Reflective Prayer –

We thank you, Lord for life, for all that you have given to those of your image. We praise you in your creations – the beauty of body and soul, of all that surrounds us, for family and friends near and far, and for nature in all its wonder and beauty.

Reflective Prayer with the Psalms

The Tenth Day ~ January 3rd

Psalm 67 begins, "O God be gracious and bless us."

"A pure heart create for me, O God, put a steadfast spirit within me." (From Psalm 51)

Reflective Prayer –

Lord, you descended to humanity to redeem us from our own inequities. Bless each soul on this earth today. Open the eyes of our hearts to your love and grace that we might turn from our desires of the flesh and worldly allurements. As we celebrate your birth on earth, lead us to our eternal life with you.

"A king is not saved by his army, nor a warrior preserved by his strength. A vain hope for safety is the horse: despite its power it cannot save.

The Lord looks on those who revere Him, on those who hope in His love, to rescue their souls from death, to keep them alive in famine…May your love be upon us O Lord, as we place all our hope in you." (From Psalm 33)

Reflective Prayer –

For Christmas

Nothing of this earth will save us for eternal life –
not money, not power, not intelligence nor the
esteem of others but the love of God alone will save
those who seek Him eternally through their lives
here, on earth. To love God is a decision and
continual act of life that sees God in all humanity.

"To you all flesh will come with its burden of sin.
Too heavy for us, our offenses, but you wipe them
away." (From Psalm 65)

Reflective Prayer –

We pray for all those poor souls who do not know
you, O Lord, our God, for those who do not believe
in you, and for those who do not know your love
and compassion.

Send forth your Holy Spirit upon them that each
may know and love you. Help us to end their loss
and confusion by your love and mercy.

Psalm 97 concludes, "Light shines forth for the just
and joy for the upright of heart. Rejoice, you just in
the Lord; give glory to His holy name."

Reflective Prayer –

Reflective Prayer with the Psalms

Justice lives in truth – the truth that is God. God,
our light, and our life   grant us your spirit of
knowledge, wisdom, and justice that we might
know the light of your joy and live in your peace.

For Christmas

The Eleventh Day ~ January 4th

"So will you be known upon earth and all nations learn your saving help." (From Psalm 67)

Psalm 8 begins, "How great is your name, O Lord our God, through all the earth!"

Reflective Prayer –

We know your saving help – your unconditional love for all of humanity. Guide our hearts and minds to love as you love every soul you create on this earth from conception through eternal life.

––––––––

"My soul is thirsting for God, the God of my life; when can I enter and see the face of God?" (From Psalm 42)

Reflective Prayer –

Our thirst for you, O Lord, cannot be understood in the terms of this world for you are beyond the world and yet reside within us. Draw us to you by your grace and keep us in your tender care as we live in this world but are not of it.

––––––––

"O God, we ponder your love within your temple. your praise, O God, like your name reaches the ends of the earth." (From Psalm 48)

Reflective Prayer with the Psalms

Reflective Prayer –

We praise your name, O Lord, our God, always!
Praise to you for our very life, for all we have, for
our families, for our gifts to share with others, and
especially for our trials and tribulations that
strengthen our souls as we face them with your
grace.

———

"You are the God who works wonders. you showed
your power among the peoples. Your strong arm
redeemed your people, the sons of Jacob and
Joseph." (From Psalm 77)

Reflective Prayer –

Grant us, O Lord, grace upon grace that we might
increase in faith. May our belief in you overshadow
all our earthly suffering and give glory to your
name. Then we will be the witness to your glory
that you ask of us. Then we will know the true
glory of your power. For we will be redeemed in
accepting your call to follow you.

For Christmas

The Twelfth Day ~ January 5th

(As Epiphany Observed)

P salm 24 begins, "The Lord's is the earth and its fullness, the world and all its peoples."

"So I gaze on you in the sanctuary to see your strength and your glory." (From Psalm 63)

Reflective Prayer –

O Lord, your strength and your glory go unseen throughout the world. Yet, this power and glory have no equal and is without end. Fill us with your grace, O Lord, that we may always do your will as the world turns from you. May we be the good stewards of the earth by first protecting and defending human life in all its stages.

———

"But my soul shall be joyful in the Lord and rejoice in His salvation. My whole being will say: 'Lord, who is like you who rescue the weak from the strong and the poor from the oppressor?'" (From Psalm 35)

Reflective Prayer –

Day by day the strong torment the weak. But you, O Lord, employ the least to shame the proud. You avoid the boastful but seek the humble and contrite heart. Gather all those who seek you into yourself for eternal joy.

————

Psalm 43 begins, "Defend me, O God, and plead my cause against a godless nation. From deceitful and cunning men rescue me. O God."

Reflective Prayer –

We seek your grace today and always, O God. Grace to withstand and endure a nation of people who have turned from you to pursue self-interest, self-importance, and self-love, thereby ignoring your truth and the needs of others. Guide us toward your love and help us attend to all who need our help.

————

Psalm 81 begins: "Ring out your joy to God our strength, shout in triumph to the God of Jacob."

Reflective Prayer –

Our Creator, you have humbled yourself to come amongst us. You were born into human life and laid in a manger from where livestock fed. In this act alone there is love beyond our understanding.

For Christmas

Yet your love is so far beyond this humbling act. In your humanity, you suffered and died that we might live eternally with You.

Guide our hearts that we might begin to grasp the great expanse of your love for us. We praise you with great joy!

Reflective Prayer with the Psalms

The Thirteenth Day ~ *(Traditional Epiphany of the Lord)* ~ January 6th

*I*t is He who set it on the seas; on the waters He made it firm. (From Psalm 24)

"Day unto day takes up the story and night unto night makes known the message." (From Psalm 19)

Reflective Prayer –

O God, our Creator, help us to know you in all you have given us; in every living thing on the earth; and, in each gift you send us in our minds and in our souls each day.

———

Psalm 67 begins, "O God be gracious and bless us and let your face shed its light upon us."

Reflective Prayer –

Lord grant us the vision of your face, an epiphany that is you – the Light of the world. Lead us in your holy way of Eucharist, your loving presence; and may we be wrapped in the Holy Spirit.

———

Psalm 121 begins, "I lift up my eyes to the mountains: from where shall come my help? My

For Christmas

help shall come from the Lord who made heaven and earth."

Reflective Prayer –

You are our help and our salvation. No gift of man can be of any value in the face of your help, your guidance, and your love, O Lord our God!

The magi came with fabulous gifts for the new-born king but, these have perished as do all gifts of the earth. You are the only everlasting joy – our Creator and Redeemer.

The Christmas Season continues to

The Baptism of the Lord ~

Reflective Prayer with the Psalms

The Fourteenth Day ~ January 7th *(On Sunday, Epiphany and The Baptism of the Lord)*

(As Epiphany Observed)

P salm 96 concludes, "Let the heavens rejoice and earth be glad, let the sea and all within it thunder praise, let the land and all it bears rejoice, all the trees of the wood shout for joy at the presence of the Lord for He comes, He comes to rule the earth. With justice He will rule the world, He will judge the peoples with His truth."

Reflective Prayer –

On this solemnity we praise you, O God, for this first appearance to gentiles: And we pray for all those who do not know you. For you are the only truth. Without you, we are confused by the very word, "truth".

———

Psalm 95 begins, "Come, let us sing to the Lord and shout with joy to the Rock who saves us."

"Blessed is he whom you choose and call to dwell in your courts." (From Psalm 65)

Reflective Prayer –

Lord, we praise you for bringing us the gift of eternal salvation! Guide us in our journey on this

For Christmas

earth: that we may see you in each soul we meet, offering your gifts to us to each other, for in such shared gifts is the joy of eternal love that brings us home to you.

———

"Lord, you have been good to your servant according to your word. Teach me discernment and knowledge for I trust in your commands." (From Psalm 119)

Reflective Prayer –

Your grace is abundant upon us, Lord. Guide us to use it for our good and the good of others. Help us to judge our own thoughts, words, and actions according to your word and give others the benefit of the doubt by showing mercy instead of judgement.

———

Psalm 135 begins, "Praise the name of the Lord, praise Him, servants of the Lord, who stand in the house of the Lord in the courts of the house of God."

Reflective Prayer –

Reflective Prayer with the Psalms

We praise you, O Lord, for your glory. You have made us out of love and redeemed us out of love.

Our Creator, you love us beyond all telling. May we ever praise you by our love for one another.

For Christmas

The Fifteenth Day ~ January 8th

"Let us approach Him with praise and thanksgiving and sing joyful songs to the Lord." (From Psalm 95)

Psalm 77 begins: "I cry aloud to God, cry aloud to God that He may hear me."

We praise you, O Lord, in times of sadness and loss, for in our suffering, we know the joy that is our gift of self. You, O Lord, love every soul you create and bring us the joy the world cannot give as we suffer and mourn for one another.

———

(Friday) Psalm 51 begins, "Have mercy on me, God, in your kindness. In your compassion blot out my offense. O wash me more and more from my guilt and cleanse me from my sin…a pure heart create in me, O God."

Reflective Prayer –

Grant us, O God, mercy, and kindness that we may show such to each other. Guide us to love and protect the least among us from the unborn to the imprisoned. May we not see others in a light of opposition but as you see each of us, your children. Guide us to love and respect our brothers and sisters who see things differently from our view.

———

Reflective Prayer with the Psalms

Psalm 97 begins: "The Lord is king, let earth rejoice, the many coastlands be glad."

Reflective Prayer –

The magi came from a foreign land to see the newborn king – a king for all people of all lands. Let us rejoice, be glad and praise His name!

Lord Jesus, you are our king our Creator and our Redeemer. Guide us to love you as you have loved us – by dying on the cross for our sins. May we show our love for you in every thought, every word, and all that we do for others.

For Christmas

The Sixteenth Day ~ January 9th

"The Lord is God, the mighty God, the great king over all the gods." (From Psalm 95)

Psalm 81 begins, "Ring out your joy to God our strength, shout in triumph to the God of Jacob."

Reflective Prayer –

There is nothing that exists that is as great as you, O Lord our God, for all that is comes from you and continues at your will. In thanksgiving for our being, we praise you and joyfully proclaim you to the world!

———

"May the Lord answer in time of trial; may the name of Jacob's God protect you...May He give you your heart's desire and fulfill every one of your plans." (From Psalm 20)

Reflective Prayer –

In his *Confessions*, St. Augustine proclaims, "Our hearts are restless until they rest in thee, O God."

Let our hearts be one with you, O Lord, that we may rest in you and know that you fill our heart's desire, and our plans are your will.

———

Reflective Prayer with the Psalms

"It is good to give thanks to the Lord, to make music to your name, O Most High ... Though the wicked spring up like grass and all who do evil thrive: they are doomed to be eternally destroyed. But you, Lord, are eternally on high." (From Psalm 92)

Reflective Prayer –

O God, our God, how glorious is your name! You have told us to seek justice and righteousness in your name. Indeed, our joy will come by living your truth. Praying for those who call evil good and good evil, we long to see your face.

For Christmas

The Seventeenth Day ~ January 10th

(Baptism of the Lord)

*H*appy the man who fears the Lord, who takes delight in all His commands ... Open-handed he gives to the poor; his justice stands firm forever. His head will be raised in glory. (From Psalm 112)

Reflective Prayer –

Lord, our God, guide us to live in your presence each moment of the day – to care for each other as your sons and daughters. May we always trust in your justice.

———

"He holds in His hands the depths of the earth and the highest mountains as well." (From Psalm 95)

"He sends out His word to the earth and swiftly runs His command." (From Psalm 147)

Yours is truth and light O Lord! Guide our hearts, minds, and souls this day to show forth your truth to the world in all we think, all we speak and all we do.

Reflective Prayer with the Psalms

The Eighteenth Day ~ January 11th

"He made the sea; it belongs to Him, the dry land too, for it was formed by His hands." (From Psalm 95)

"O Lord, how great are your works! How deep are your designs! The foolish man cannot know this and the fool cannot understand." (From Psalm 92)

Reflective Prayer –

O Lord, our God, Creator of every human soul from conception through all eternity, you have given us dominion over all earthly creation. Yet how basely we have treated your work, even destroying that which you created in your own image and likeness while still in the womb.

O loving Father have mercy on your greatly loved creation. Guide every soul on the earth to your love that we may turn from our abuses and begin again to be the good and loving stewards of all your earthly creations.

"Lead me, Lord, in your justice, because of those who lie in wait; make clear your way before me." (From Psalm 5)

For Christmas

Reflective Prayer –

Guide us in your truth, O Lord, that we might live in and according to the truth that is you. Create a pure heart in us, Lord, that we may seek justice for all.

Reflective Prayer with the Psalms

The 19th Day ~ January 12th

(Baptism of the Lord)

*C*ome, then, let us bow down and worship, bending the knee before the Lord our maker. (From Psalm 95)

Reflective Prayer –

O Lord, our God, you revealed to us your divine nature in your own baptism. Help us to remember that we died to sin in our baptism and rise to new life in you.

As we live in you and you in us, may we never offend you in each other but always see and minister to you, living in one another.

———

"Our soul is waiting for the Lord. The Lord is our help and our shield." (From Psalm 33)

Reflective Prayer –

Lord, guide us and protect us from a world that does not know you. Bless us in our sufferings and sacrifices for you in others and for your name's sake. May we always be joyful in our sorrows and sufferings.

For Christmas

January 13th *(Latest possible day of the Baptism of the Lord Solemnity)*

P salm 36 begins, "Sin speaks to the sinner in the depths of his heart. There is no fear of God before his eyes.

He so flatters himself in his mind that he knows not his guilt. In his mouth are mischief and deceit. All wisdom is gone."

Reflective Prayer –

Guide us Lord, in your wisdom. Lead us to you in faith so that we trust in you and you alone. Help us to turn from our selfish desires and guide us to the love of you – that we see you in every soul we meet.

———

"Go up, Lord, to the place of your rest, you and the ark of your strength. Your priests shall be clothed with holiness: your faithful shall ring out their joy." (From Psalm 132)

Reflective Prayer –

We shout for joy in your presence, O Lord! You are in the line of David, servant of God, yet you are King of the earth and heaven. May your praise be always on our lips and your joy always in our hearts.

Reflective Prayer with the Psalms

FROM THE AUTHOR

Reflective Prayer with the Psalms

About the Author

John Paul Benage is an ordained Catholic deacon in the Archdiocese of San Antonio, Texas, who serves the people of God at St. Peter Prince of the Apostles parish. Deacon John Paul has previously published a novel titled, *Oak* Grove. The second edition of this novel was published in 2019. He also serves the Catholic Community Foundation, assisting with planned and estate giving as well as endowments.

Oak Grove and *Reflective Prayer with the Psalms* are available on Amazon.com.

From the Author

A Note:

Did you enjoy *Reflective Prayer with the Psalms*? If yes, it would mean so much to me if you take a moment to submit a review on Amazon. Also, since a self-published author's best marketing strategy is word of mouth, please share how much you enjoyed this little book with others. Your love and support for this book are much appreciated.

John Paul Benage